THE
COLLECTED WORKS
OF
WILLIAM BYRD

Edited by

EDMUND H. FELLOWES

VOLUME XIX

KEYBOARD WORKS (Part ii.)

LONDON :

STAINER & BELL LTD.

69 NEWMAN STREET, OXFORD STREET, W.1

1950

MADE IN ENGLAND

PREFACE TO VOLUME XIX

THIS volume contains the whole of the collected pavans and galliards. These two dance-forms, so commonly associated together by the Tudor composers, were both of them ordinarily constructed in three sections, consisting, in the case of the pavan, of strains of eight, sixteen, and sometimes as many as thirty-two bars, each of which was followed by a " reprise ", that is to say a variation, or elaboration of the preceding strain, and having the same number of bars. The sections of the galliards were normally half the length of those of the pavans. The pavan was a stately dance-form in duple measure, and the galliard was in triple measure.

The arrangement and numbering of the pieces in this volume is arbitrary, except that the first ten pavans with their galliards are those so numbered in the Nevell book. The seventh and eighth pavan have no galliard. Apart from the grouping of these pavans and galliards as ten single units, each piece is also numbered as a separate composition as in the Nevell book, both in the headings and in the table of contents.

In the present volume all the pairs of pavans and galliards are numbered as single units.

CONTENTS

*N = My Ladye Nevells Booke.   Edited by Hilda Andrews.
F = The Fitzwilliam Virginal Book, edited by J. A. Fuller Maitland and W. Barclay Squire.
T = William Byrd, Forty-five pieces for keyboard instruments, edited by Stephen D. Tuttle.
P = Parthenia 1611.

NOTES

1. The Firste Pavian and Galliarde

Nevell 10, 11 ; *Fitzwilliam* 167, 168 ; *Drexel* 5612, *p.* 132, 134

PAVAN

(7) tenor, 4th beat, add A : Fitz.; bass. semibreve : Fitz. (8) BC for first B : Fitz. (10) ♭ : om Fitz. (15) and (31) ties : added. (18) treble. D dotted with crotchet : Drex. (22) 1st beat. ♮ : om Drex. (23) lh. ♮ : om Drex. (24) add ♮ to E and ♯ to F : Fitz. (25) rh. ♮ : om Fitz. and Drex. (26) lh. ♭ : om Fitz.; rh. ♭ : added.

(27) alto C : om N and Drex. (31) rh. 1st beat. ♯ : om Drex.; ♮ to E : added ; alto.

: Drex. (34) tenor. A B (crotchet) A for BA : Fitz. (38) alto. F♮ dotted and C (crotchet) : Fitz. (40) A for C : Fitz. (45) add ♯ to C : N and Fitz.; lh. add ♮ to B and E : Fitz. (47) add ♮ to E : Drex. (50) lh. D for E : N. (54) C : octave lower. (56) A for B : Fitz. (60) tenor. F. semibreve for minim : N. (63) 3rd beat : Nevell text obscured and corrected in a later hand. (69) ♯ : om N. (71) 2nd beat. C : om N ; D for C : Fitz. and Drex. (cf bar 87). (78) tenor. DC (crotchets) D (minim) : Fitz. (95) rh. ♮ to E : om N and Fitz.; ♮ to B : om Fitz and Drex. (96) ♮ to E and B : om N ; ♮ to B : om Fitz and Drex.

GALLIARD

(12) rh. add ♮ to E : Fitz. (13) lh. add ♮ to E : Drex. (15) add ♮ to B and ♯ to F : Drex.; 3rd beat. add ♮ to E : Fitz. (16) ♮ : om N and Drex. (21) rh. add ♮ to E : Fitz. (22) alto. A dotted and BAG (crotchets) : Fitz. and Drex. (25) rh. ♮ : om N ; ♭ marked : Fitz. (27) rh. ♮ to B : om N ; ♮ to E : om N and Fitz. (30) 3rd beat. G for A : Fitz. (32) lh. ♮ : om N and Fitz. (34) alto. last note. G : N, (36) and (44) lh. ♮ : om N. (39) alto. E minim for EC : N.

2. The Seconde Pavian and Galliarde

Nevell 12, 13 ; *Fitzwilliam* 257, 258 ; *BM Add.* 30485. *f.6* ; *Forster f.59v, 122v*

PAVAN

Described as Pavana Fant(asia) in the Fitzwilliam manuscript. The pavan and galliard are placed independently in the Forster manuscript.

(1) add dot to G and om rest : For. (12) lh. ♯ : om Fitz. (19) 3rd beat. rest for B : N. (24) tenor. ♭ : om BM. (25) 4th beat. D : om N. (29) 1st beat. add ♯ to F : BM. and For.; 1st and 2nd beats, semiquavers a third higher : Fitz. and For. (30) rh. ♯ : om N. BM. and For. (31) rh. 1st beat. ♭ : om BM. and For.; ♯ : om Fitz. (39) 4th beat. AB for BA : BM. and For. (42) ♯ to F : added ; 4th beat AG (quavers) : BM. (44) 3rd beat. add ♯ to C : Fitz. and BM. (44) (49) and (50) 4th beat eight demisemiquavers : N.

GALLIARD

The sections of this galliard are, by exception, of the same length as those of the pavan.

(4) lh. D (minim) : om Fitz. (6) rh. CB : om N and For. (8) text as in bar 16 : For. (16) rh. 3rd beat. E for D : N. (17) 2nd beat. add ♯ to F (bis) : Fitz.; 3rd beat. add ♯ to G (bis) : Fitz. (19) to (22) ♩♩♩ for ♩. ♪♩ passim : N. (23) 3rd beat. alto (E (minim) for FDE : N. (25) rh. add ♯ to G : Fitz. and For. (26) ♯ to G : om Fitz and For. (29) (31) and (32) 3rd beat. eight demisemiquavers : N., BM. and For. (31) 2nd beat. C.D : om Fitz., and inserted in a later hand : N. (42) tenor D for 2nd B : BM. and For.

3. The Third Pavian and Galliarde

Nevell 14, 15 ; *Fitzwilliam* 252, 253 ; *BM. Add.* 30485. *f.1, 3* ; 31392 (*wanting bars* 1—20) ; *Drexel* 5612. *p.* 62, 64

PAVAN

(13) alto. AG (crotchets) for A (minim) : N. (19) A for rest : BM.1. (22)   BM1.

and Drex. (cf. bar 20). (25) 3rd beat. G for low E: Fitz.; ♯ to G: om Drex. (29) 4th beat C for G: Fitz., BM1. and Drex. (30) 1st and 2nd group a third lower: N. (31) 1st beat. C: om Drex.; ♯: om N. and BM2. (37) and (38) rh. semibreves: N. and BM2. (44) alto. G (minim): om Fitz.;  : Fitz

(46) 1st beat. two quavers E for crotchet: BM2. (51) ♯ to 1st G: om N and Drex. (53) rh. G semibreve: N. and BM2. (54) F, GF for F (crotchet): Fitz. (59) and (60) ♯ to F: om BM2. (61) add ♯ to G (bis): Drex.; lh. add ♯ to G: Fitz. (63) For variants see below. (73) alto. 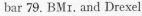 : Fitz., BM1. and Drex. (75) tenor. as in bar 73. (79) For variants see below. (80) add ♯ to G: Fitz. (81) ♯ to F: om Fitz (bis). (83) tenor. 1st C. add ♯: Fitz. (85) D (quaver): om N. and BM1. (87) ♯ to F: om Fitz., BM2. and Drex.; C redundant: Fitz. (89) ten quavers for semiquavers: N. (90) ♯: om Fitz.; add ♯ to C: BM2. (91) rh. ♯: om N., Fitz and BM1. (92) DA (crotchets) for C (minim): Fitz. (93) 4th beat all a third higher: Fitz. (94) and (95) For variants see below

bars 63 and 64. Fitzwilliam

bar 63. BM1 and Drexel

bar 79. BM1. and Drexel

bars 94-97. Fitzwilliam

bars 95-96. BM1. and Drexel

GALLIARD

(1) to (2) dotted crotchet and quaver for crotchets (bis): Fitz. and Drex. (10) 1st note, rest for A: N. (19) E (semibreve) for EC: N and BM2. (21) [music] : N and BM2; C (tenor) for E: N. and BM2. (23) [music] and tenor. om ♯ to C: Fitz., BM1. and Drex. (24) 1st beat. rh. dotted crotchet and quaver for A minim: Drex. (27) 3rd beat DEFD (quavers): Fitz. (31) lh. ♯: om N., BM.1, BM2 and Drex. (32) ♯ to F: om Fitz., BM2. and Drex; ♯ to G: added. (37) [music] Fitz. and Drex. (38) tenor 3rd beat A (minim): N. (39) tenor 1st beat D for CD: N. (41) to (49) For variants see below.

bars 41-49. Fitzwilliam, BM1. and Drexel

4. THE FOURTH PAVIAN AND GALLIARDE
Nevell 16, 17 ; *BM. Add* 30485. *f.81v., 83v*

PAVAN

(5) alto. F (dotted) for CF : N. (6) G (dotted) F : om N. (11) rh. 4th beat. F (crotchet) : N. (15) 1st beat. E : om BM.; lh. 3rd beat crotchet rest and G quaver for semi-quaver : N. (19) rh. B (minim) for BC : N. (23) 1st beat. add dot to C♯ : N. (28) tenor. 1st beat. E : om N ; 2nd beat. C (crotchet) for DC : N. (30) rh. 2nd and 3rd beats. ♯ : added. (33) rh. 1st beat. crotchet for minim : N (34) ♯ to F : om N. (41) 1st C. semi-

quaver for quaver : N. (42) ♯ to C : om N ; lh.  : N. (43) lh. ♯ : added (bis). (44) lh. 3rd and

4th beats [notation] : BM.

GALLIARD

(3) tenor. D for C : N. (8) lh. 3rd beat. G for C : BM. (15) see below. (19) lh. 1st beat. two crotchets : N. (25) lh. last two notes. EF : BM. (34) rh. add ♯ to G : N. (42) tenor. 2nd and 3rd beats. add C (minim) AB (crotchets) : BM. (43) tenor. GA : om N.

bar 15. BM.

[musical notation]

5. THE FIFTE PAVIAN AND GALLIARDE
Nevell 18, 19 ; *BM. Add* 31392. *f.3v, 5v ; Drexel* 5612. p. 136, 138

PAVAN

(6) ♮ : om BM. and Drex. (9) add F♯ : Drex. (13) 1st three beats [notation] : Drex.

(20) rh. ♮ : om Drex. (21) 2nd beat. DC for D : Drex. (22) tenor. [notation] : BM. (26) alto. E : om

N. and BM. (29)—(30) see below. (31) 1st and 2nd beats. ♮ : added (bis). (33) dotted minim for AGA : Drex. (36) D (minim) for DCD : Drex. (39) 1st beat. F♯ (crotchet) : Drex. (47) 3rd beat. ♮ : om Drex. (48) add ♮ to E : BM. and Drex. (51) tenor. DCBA (crotchets) : BM. and Drex. (51)—(52) see below. (54) 1st two beats. GABC, DBCD : BM. (61) tenor, semiquavers for quavers : N.; bass. C : om BM. (62) 3rd beat. ♮ to E : om BM. (63) ♮ : om BM. (bis). (65) tenor. DC for EB : BM. (71) dot to G, and A (crotchet) : N. and Drex.

(72) CD : om N and Drex. (73) DE for CD : Drex. (79) [notation] : BM. (81) add ♮ to B :

Drex. (83) rh. ♭ : om N.; ♮ for ♭ : Drex.; lh. semiquavers for quavers : N. (88) CD : om N. and BM. (95) lh. add ♮ to B (bis) : BM.

bars 29-30. Drexel   bars 51-52. BM.

GALLIARD
(9) rh. for ♭ : Drex. (15) lh. ♮ to E : om BM. (19) ♯ : om Drex. (20) alto. [music] : Drex; [music] : BM. (22) 3rd beat. add ♮ to E : BM. (26) 1st beat. ♮ to B : om N. and BM. (27) ♯ to F and ♮ to E : om BM. and Drex. (28) ♮ to E : om BM.; ♯ to F : om N. and BM. (33) ♮ to B : om BM. (35) ♮ to B : om BM. and Drex. (38) alto. last note D for C : BM. (43) rh. ♮ : om Drex. (44) rh. ♮ : om N. ; 3rd. beat. add ♭ to E : N. (46) rh. last note. E : N. (48) ♮ to E : om Drex.; ♮ to B : om N.

6. Pavana the Sixte and Galliarde
"Kinbrugh (Kinlough) : goodd"
Nevell 20, 21 ; BM. Add. 30485. f. 22, 23 ; 31392 f. 9v, 11v

The name "Kinbrugh", as found in the Nevell book is a misreading of "Kinlough". The error may go back to an earlier transcription. Among the Panmure MSS. at Carnoustie (c 1600—15), are several virginal pieces by William Kinloch, probably a member of the old Angus family of Kinloch, and presumably identical with "Mr. Kinloughe", a pavan and galliard by whom are in the BM. Add. MS. 30485.

It was a common habit with Byrd to associate the dedicatory name of a friend with a composition like this ; for example : "Mr. W. Peter", "The Earle of Salisbury", and "Miss Marye Brownlo".

The colon inserted between the words "Kinbrugh" and "goodd" in the Nevell book was omitted in the published edition, and "goodd" is printed with a capital G. It was an ordinary practice at this period, when checking the text of a newly-transcribed manuscript to endorse it with such words as "true", or "good", at the conclusion, to certify its accuracy. Although in an un-usual position, that is the meaning of the word here.

PAVAN
(11) bass C : om BM2 ; tenor. A for B : BM2. (12) alto. G : om N. (14) 4th beat. demisemiquavers : N ; B (crotchet) : BM2. (27) tenor. A for B : BM2. (28) 4th beat. CABC : BM1. (43) tenor. FG (crotchets) : BM1. (52) tenor. 3rd beat. C for D : N. (55) alto. G for rest : BM1. (56) add ♯ to F : BM2. (61) add ♯ to C : N. and BM2. (78) ♭ : om BM2. (80) rh. quaver for crotchet : N. (94) to (96) eight demisemi for six semiquaver groups : N. (97) tenor. B for C : N.

GALLIARD
(11) rh. 3rd beat. A for G : BM1. (12) bass. G : om BM2. (13) rh. 2nd beat. GF (quavers) : BM2. (23) 3rd beat. F (minim) : BM2. (25) alto. 3rd beat. G. (crotchet) AG (quavers) : BM1. (31) 3rd beat. eight semiquavers: BM1. and BM2. (39) alto. E for F : BM1. (45) lh. ♭ : om BM2.

7. The Seventh Pavian
(Pavana Canon)
Nevell 22 ; Fitzwilliam 275

In the Fitzwilliam book this is called "Pavana Canon" for the reason that the alto part is in strict canon with the treble. The canon can be traced fairly clearly in the more florid passages. No galliard is associated with this Pavan.

(1) add ♯ to F : Fitz. (10) ♯ : om Fitz. (12) ♮ : om N. (17) 1st beat. add ♯ to F : Fitz. 3rd beat. add ♮ to F : Fitz. (28) 3rd beat. add ♮ to C : Fitz.; 4th beat. ♮ : om N. (31) ♯ : om Fitz. (32) ♯ : added. (35) ♯ to F : om N. (42) ♯ to G : om Fitz. (53) CB. wrongly altered in later hand to dotted crotchet and quaver : N. (cf. alto in bar 55 and Fitz.). (58) alto D : om N. (62) tenor ♯ : om Fitz. (63) 3rd beat. semi-quavers : N.; E for G on seventh note : N. (66) ♭ : added. (72) CD (crotchets) : Fitz. (81) ♭ : om Fitz. (82) ♭ : added (cf. bar 66). (86) D (minim) : om Fitz.; and misplaced on the 3rd beat : N. (cf alto. bar 88). (91) tenor. B for A : N. (93) ♯ : om N.

8. The Eighte Pavian

Nevell 23

No galliard is associated with this pavan.

(24) 3rd beat. ♯: om N. (30) 4th beat. demisemiquavers: N. (49 and 50) 4th beat. semiquavers: N. (54) 4th beat. demisemiquavers: N. (62) alto. A for G: N. (79) ♯ to G: om N. (92) 1st beat. ♯: om N (bis). (95) lh. ♯: om N.

9. The Nynthe Pavian and Galliarde

"The Passinge mesures", or "Passamezzo"

Nevell 24, 25; *Fitzwilliam* 56, 57; BM. *Add.* 30486. *f.*7, 11; 31392 (*lute, pavan only*); *Forster. f.*111, 117*v.* *Panmure* (*Kinloch*) *No.* 12.

The two conventional dance measures are here designed on a scheme four times the normal length. Each of the three sections of the pavan consists of sixty-four bars, half of which, in strains of eight bars each, represent the first statement, to be followed by a corresponding reprise. This pavan thus contains as many as 192 bars. The sections of the galliard are just half this length.

The meaning of the term Passamezzo, or Passing measures remains uncertain. Byrd was not alone in using it, and other examples are of similar design. The suggestion that each movement was intended to be played faster as the pieces progressed, or that the whole composition was played faster than the ordinary pavans and galliards, cannot be supported on the internal evidence of the note-values.

PAVAN

(1) rh. rest om, and G dotted: Fitz., BM. and Pan. (9) ♯: om BM. and For. (22) 2nd group. GABG: N. and Pan. (27) rh. EF for AB: Fitz. BM. and Pan. (28) For variants see below. (31) 2nd and 3rd beats. quavers:

N.; 3rd and 4th beats  : Fitz., BM. and Pan. (37) tenor. AB: om N. (42) ♯: om Fitz.,

BM. and Pan. (44) 3rd and 4th beat. CDBC: Pan. (48) 2nd beat. crotchet rest for quaver: N. (53) bass. semibreve for minim: N. (55) rh. last note. C for D: For. (58) ♯ to F: om Fitz. and Pan. (69) alto A: om N. (79) ♯ to C: om Fitz., For. and Pan. (82) and (86) 4th beat. demisemiquavers: N. (84) rh. 1st beat. two

quavers: Fitz. and For. 1st and 2nd beat  : BM. (88) ♮: om BM. (bis); bass. quavers for

semi quavers: N. (89) 1st note. semiquaver for quaver: N.; 2nd beat. CD for GA: Fitz. BM., For and Pan. (90) last five notes. a third lower: Fitz. and BM. (91) to (92) For variants see below. (92) 4th beat. demisemi-quavers: N. (94) lh. ♮ and ♯: om Fitz., BM. and For. (99) minim for dotted crotchet quavers: Pan. (100) rh. wrong values: Pan. (107) G. (dotted crotchet) for GFG: Fitz., BM. and Pan. (109) FG (crotchets) for quavers: Fitz. (110) F (crotchet): om Fitz. (118) GAB for FGA: N. and Pan. (123) ♯s: om Fitz.; FG for 1st AB: Fitz., BM. and Pan. (125) CD for GA: Fitz.; (125) and (126) for variants see below. (145) alto. F: om N. and Pan. (154) rh. D (quaver): N. (155) and (156) add ♮ to B: N. (158) and (159) ♮ to B: om Fitz. and For. (174) C♯ and bass: trs up an octave. (176) A for F♮: N. and Fitz.; ♭ to 1st E: om N. (178) rh. G for F: Fitz.; E for F: BM. (181) 3rd beat. E for C (semi-quaver): Fitz. BM. and Pan. (182) similarly D for B, and C for A: Fitz., BM. and Pan. (186) For variants see below. (188) 3rd beat. FGE: om N.; and six demisemi-for semiquavers: N.; and for variant see below. (190) 1st beat. C for A: Pan. (193) bass. F for G: N.

bar 28. Fitzwilliam, BM. and Panmure

bars 91 and 92. Fitzwilliam and Panmure   bars 91 and 92. BM.

bars 125 and 126. BM. and Panmure

bar 126. Fitzwilliam

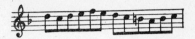

bars 185 and 186. Fitzwilliam, BM. and Panmure

bar 188. Fitzwilliam, BM. and Panmure

bar 188 3rd and 4th beat. Nevell.

GALLIARD

The Nevell and Forster manuscripts have a second reprise at the end of the second section. In the Nevell book a second flat appears in the signature from bars 1 to 80 and from 93 to 112 in both staves ; and from 85 to 87 in lower stave only. How far these signatures take effect is not always certain. There is no second flat in the signatures of the Fitzwilliam, the British Museum, Forster or Panmure manuscripts. There are very few accidentals in the Panmure manuscript and no ornaments. The accidentals in Panmure are not noted here.

(12) tenor. A : om Fitz., BM. and Pan. ; bass. G : om N. (32) lh. add ♯ to F : Fitz and BM. (38) D (semibreve) for D (dotted) CB : Fitz.; bass. A. semibreve minim : Pan. (40) whole bar omitted : N. (41) lh. chord of D for B♭ : N. apparently taken from the omitted bar. (48) tenor. crotchets a third too low : For. (50) tenor. ♮ : om N. and BM.; and see below. (51) 2nd beat FE : om, and FG crotchets for quavers : Fitz. (61) to (63) see below. (64) lh. six quavers : om Fitz. and BM. (65) to (80) This section is omitted in Fitz., BM. and Pan. (70) alto. GF for FE : N. (82) (83) and (84). dotted crotchet and two semiquavers for crotchet and two quavers : Fitz and BM. (94) rh. A : om BM. and Pan. (110) lh. ♯ to F : om BM. (127) ♯ to F : om Fitz. (132) lh.: trs up an octave. (140) rh. 3rd beat. F minim : Fitz. and Pan. (141) rh. ED (minims) for D, and B (minim) for AB : Fitz., BM. and Pan. ; tenor. add ♮ to B : For.

bar 50 Fitzwilliam. BM. and Panmure   bars 61-63 Fitzwilliam. BM. and Panmure

10. THE TENNTHE PAVIAN AND GALLIARDE
"Mr. W. Peter"

Parthenia 2, 3 ; Nevell 39, 40 ; BM. Add 30486. f. 14, 16 ; Forster f. 157, 160v.; Drexel 50612. p. 100 (pavan only)

Sir William Petre was one of Byrd's personal friends and patrons. He was one of the principal Secretaries of State in the reigns of Henry VIII and Elizabeth. His son John Petre was also Byrd's friend. He was created Lord Petre of Writtle.

PAVAN

(8) lh. ♮ : om BM. (10) ♮ : om BM. and Drex. (13) rh. ♮ : om Drex. (16) ♮ to E : om Parth, N. and Drex. (17) E. add ♮ (bis) : N. (23) ♮ : om N, For and Drex. (24) lh. F : om N, BM. and For. (26) lh. 1st beat. F : om Parth. and Drex. (27) ♮ to C : om Drex. (28) 1st beat. ♮ : om BM. and For.; last note. ♮ : om Parth and Drex. (29) 2nd beat. ♮ : om BM. and Drex. (30) ♮ to B : om BM and For.; 3rd and 4th beats. quavers for semi-quavers: For. (31) all accidentals : om BM. and Drex. (36) rests for dots : N. (40) alto. D for ED : For.; add ♯ to C : N. (41) tenor. D : om BM. (42) tenor. A (quaver) for crotchet : N (44) ♯ : om Drex.; ♮ : om N and Drex. (45) ♮ : om For. (46) 4th beat. eight semiquavers : N. (47) 3rd beat. D (semiquaver) : N. (49) add ♮ to E : Parth. (51) rh. ♮ : om Parth and BM. (52) ♮ to E : om N. (55) rh. 1st beat. a third lower : Drex.; 3rd beat F (quaver) for FE : Parth. and N.; lh. B (minim) for BA : Parth. BM., For. and Drex. (57) lh. 3rd beat ♯ : om N and For. (59) 4th beat. B : om N. (60) lh. 4th beat. add ♮ to B : BM. (77) alto. D for DE ; N.; alto. the whole bar : om For. (77) and (78) semiquavers : Parth. (87) 3rd beat. G (crotchet) BM. and For.; lh. 2nd beat. AF (quavers): BM. and For. (93) lh. ♮ (bis) : om N. and Drex. (94) 4th beat. demisemiquavers: N. (95) to (99) see below.

bars 95 to 99. Nevell, BM. and Forster

bars 95 to 97. Parthenia and Drexel

GALLIARD

(5) add ♯ to F : For. (6) bass. last note. D for E : For. (11) E (minim) : om Parth. (24) alto. DC : om N. (39) 3rd beat. GE for EG : Parth and For. (42) rh. 3rd beat. crotchet A for quaver : N ; F and C : om N ; tenor. AC (as in bar 41) : N. (43) tenor. : om Parth. (45) alto. F (crotchet) : om N. (46) 3rd beat. values apparently halved : all sources ; but A (quaver) is correct in N only. (47) to (50) note-values are apparently halved in all sources (including Parthenia and Nevell) except in the 3rd beat of bar 48. (49) The quaver rest appears correctly in Nevell only.

11. PAVANA AND GALIARDA
"Bray"
Fitzwilliam 91, 92

PAVAN
(18) F for G : Fitz. (55) bass. possibly add dot to F, and E (crotchet). (cf bar 39).

GALLIARD
(5) and (6) alto : trs up from tenor. (41) rh. add ♯ to F : Fitz.

12. PAVANA AND GALIARDO
"The Earle of Salisbury"
Parthenia 6; 7 ; *Drexel, p.* 60, 61

13. PAVANA AND GALLIARD
"Ph. Tr (egian)"
Fitzwilliam 93, 94 ; *Bull f.*88*v* (pavan only) : *Drexel.* 5612. *p.* 16 (*ascr to Morley*)

PAVAN
(5) add ♮ to E : Fitz. (10) lh. G : om Fitz. (14) and (15) semi for demisemiquavers : Bull. (49) rh. 3rd beat. add ♯ to F : Fitz. (55) ♮ to B : om Fitz and Bull. (61) ♭ : om Fitz and Bull. (66) and (68) BG. semiquavers and rest : Bull. (69) G : om Fitz. (71) lh. last note. F for E : Fitz. (72) lh. whole bar missing : Fitz. (73) rh. whole bar missing : Fitz. (76) bass. C. semibreve for minim : Fitz. (79) tenor. F (minim) FC (crotchets) : Fitz. and Drex. (83) rh. 1st beat F/C : om Fitz. (87) rh. 2nd beat. GA for EF : Bull ; lh. D : om Bull. (89) 2nd beat : eight semiquavers : Bull and Drex. (92) tenor. crotchet for minim : Fitz. (94) add ♮ to B : Fitz. (94) to (96) four semi for demisemiquavers : Fitz.

GALLIARD
(4) 3rd beat. F : om Fitz. (8) lh. low F : crotchet for quaver ; and C. quaver for crotchet : Fitz. (17) ♯ : om Fitz. (18) ♮ : om Fitz. (19) rh. add ♯ to F : Drex. (23) rh. ♯ and ♮ : om Drex.; lh. AC. crotchets : Drex. (26) rh. ♯ : om Drex. (30) rh. ♮ : om Drex. (34) 3rd beat. F for G : Fitz. (36) 1st beat. ♭ : om Drex.; lh. ♮ : om Drex. (44) ♭ : om Drex. (47) 1st beat. D : om Fitz.

14. THE QUADRAN PAVEN AND GALIARD
Fitzwilliam 133, 134 ; *BM. Add.* 30485. *f.*18, 20 ; 31392. *f.*20*v*, 21*v* (*lute*) ; *Forster p.* 145. 152

The term "Quadran" may perhaps have reference to the fact that the pavan is designed in four sections as compared with the conventional three. The first and third sections consist of 32 bars, each, with a reprise following them. The second and fourth sections are of half that length. The galliard is of corresponding design, but is, as usual, half the length of the pavan, with sections of sixteen and eight bars and the customary reprise. The pavan and galliard together have a total of 340 bars.

There are many undoubted errors in all three sources of the text, especially in the Fitzwilliam book. The Forster and British Museum text are mainly identical, even in the matter of errors. The version given here of bars 20, 44, 52 and 53 is submitted as no more than a tentative suggestion.

PAVAN

(7) ♯ : om BM. (8) lh. add ♯ to F : BM. (15) tenor. add ♯ to F : BM. (18) 4th beat. eight demisemiquavers : and similarly in succeeding phrases : Fitz. (19) tenor. BCDE (quavers) for DE : Fitz. and For. (20) See below, and cf the corresponding bar 52. (24) lh. add ♯ to F : BM. (26) alto. 3rd beat. D : om BM. (35) rh. 3rd and 4th beats. add BC : Fitz. (40) add ♯ to F : Fitz. and BM. (43) 2nd beat. ♯ : om BM. and For. (44) rh. 1st beat. alto. G for EF : BM.; 4th beat. G for A ; Fitz.; lh. tenor C♮ in all sources clashing with rh.; F for A : Fitz. (45) alto. add quaver rest, and last note. quaver for crotchet : Fitz. (46) tenor. F for FG : Fitz. (47) tenor. 1st beat. GA for A : Fitz. (48) tenor. 3rd beat. ♯ to F : om Fitz. (52) and (53) the bass of these two bars interchanged, and that of 53 transposed up a fifth : Fitz. (see below). (55) rh. ED (crotchets) : Fitz. and BM. (58) ♯ : om Fitz. (64) add ♯ to C (bis) : BM. and For.; G for rest : Fitz. (68) rh. ♯ to F and C : om Fitz. (79) last five-notes. a third lower : Fitz. (83) 1st beat. add ♯ to C (bis), and tenor. A for rest : BM. and For.; G for rest : Fitz. (84) tenor. 1st beat. add ♯ to C : BM. and For. (85) 2nd beat. ♯ to C : om BM. and For. (89) lh. 2nd note. E for G : BM. (104) 1st beat. two quavers : Fitz. (108) lh. ♯ : om Fitz. (113) tenor. 2nd note. E : Fitz. (114) and (115) lh. 3rd and 4th beats. quavers : For. (117) to (120) 3rd beat. semiquavers for quavers : Fitz. (123) to (124) see below. (131) bass. dot to G, and FE (quavers) : Fitz. (132) bass. G for F : Fitz. (136) ♭ : om BM. and For. (144) DC (crotchets) : Fitz. (151) alto. 1st beat. add E (minim) : BM. and For. (156) rh. B for C : Fitz.; tenor. FG (quavers) for F : Fitz. (157) alto. C for B : BM. (158) 1st beat. C for D ; BM. and For. (168) D for C (minim) : Fitz. (178) ♯ to F : om Fitz. (179) to (181) three bars omitted : BM. and For. (182) ♯ to F : om BM. and For. (184) D (minim), F (crotchet) : Fitz.; alto. last note. G : Fitz. (188) 3rd beat. add ♯ to F : BM. (189) add ♯ to F (passim) : BM. and For. (192) lh. the whole bar : om Fitz.

bar 20. Fitzwilliam bars 52 to 53. Fitzwilliam bars 123 and 124. Fitzwilliam

GALLIARD

(6) C (minim) for semiquavers : BM. and For. (16) ♯ : om Fitz. and For. (60) ♯ : om Fitz. (61) alto. 1st beat. F for G : Fitz. (64) alto. ED : om BM. and For. (72) lh. 2nd note. C for D : BM. and For. (75) ♭ : om BM. and For. (78) lh. insert A after 2nd note and om final A : Fitz. (79) and (80) ♯ to F : om BM. and For. (86) tenor. 1st beat. add C (♮) : all sources. (91) 1st beat. F trs. up an octave. (103) rh. rest for D (minim) : Fitz. (104) lh. ♯ to F : om Fitz. (108) alto. all a beat too early : Fitz. (121) rh. D and G : added. (136) tenor. ♯ : added. (139) 1st beat. D for F : Fitz.; add ♭ to B : BM. and For. (140) add ♯ to F (bis) : BM. and For. (142) to 143) ♯ to F (passim,) : om Fitz. (144) lh. five quavers a note too high : Fitz. (145) to (146) see-below.

bar 145-147. Fitzwilliam bar 145-147. Forster

15. PAVANA AND GALLIARDA in Gam ut
Fitzwilliam 165, 166
PAVAN

(9) ♯ : om Fitz. (15) rh. last note. B for C : Fitz. (23) there have been erasures in the MS. and the text is uncertain. cf bar 46 and see below. (28) A : added. (44) ♯ to F : added. cf bar 36. (47) ♯ to F : om Fitz.

bar 23, Fitzwilliam

(43) add ♮ to B : Fitz. (cf bar 47).

16. PAVEN AND GALIARD in Gam ut
BM. Add. 30485. f.79v., 80v.

PAVAN

(7) lh. ♯ to F : added. (8) rh. ♯ to F : added. (14) lh. ♯ : added. (50) rh. ♯ : added. (55) lh. ♯ : added.

GALLIARD

(15) lh. ♯ to F : added. (21) ♯ to F (bis) : added, as in bar 29. (23) and (31) ♯ to 1st C : added. (39) rh. ♯ to F : added. (45) lh. ♯ to F : added.

17. PAVION AND GALLIARD in Gam ut
BM. Add. 30485. f.2, 3 ; Drexel. 5612. p. 16 (pavan only)

PAVAN

(22) lh. ♯ : added. (25) ♯ : om BM. (31) ♯ : om BM. (46) alto. ♯ to 1st G : om BM. (49) tenor. 1st beat. add B : Drex. (82) rh. ♭ : om BM. (83) ♭ : om BM (bis).

GALLIARD

(5) 2nd beat. C (dotted), D (quaver) : BM. (13) rh. ♯ : added. (cf. bar 5). (29) ♯ : added. (47) This bar is missing in the manuscript. It is reconstructed and added here to correspond with bar 39, and so to complete the eight-bar strain.

18. PAVANA AND GALLIARDA in A re
Fitzwilliam 173, 174 ; Drexel 5609 p. 132 (galliard only)

PAVAN

This pavan is of unusual construction. The first and second sections each consist of sixteen bars and have no reprise. It may have been intended that they should be repeated. The third section contains three strains of eight bars each, also without reprise.
(9) tenor. G (semibreve), for minim and rest : Fitz. (18) tenor. B (semibreve), for minim and rest : Fitz. (34) to (37) ♭ (passim) : om Fitz. (49) alto. A (minim), for AG : Fitz. (50) alto. G (crotchet), F♯ (minim), E (crotchet) : Fitz.

GALLIARD

(9) ♯ to F : om Fitz. (13) A for G (quaver) : Fitz. (14) rh. ♯ to C : added.

19. PAVYN AND GALIARD in A re
BM. Add. 31392. f.6v, 8v
PAVAN

(17) ♯ to G : added as in bar 1. (22) ♯ to F and G : om BM. (62) text here amended from

 (73) (81) and (89) lh. ♯ : added.

GALLIARD

(15) four ♯'s : om BM. (cf. bar 7). (28) ♯ to G : om BM. (40) ♯ to G and F : om BM. (46) rh. last note. C : BM.

20. PAVON AND GALLIARD in A re
Drexel 5612. p. 66, 68
PAVAN

(23) rh. ♯ to C : om Drex. (34) bass. low A : this note is very rarely found in the virginal writings. See also bar 46, and in the galliard bars 36, 42 and 56. (36) 1st and 3rd beats. ♯ to C and D : om Drex. (37) 2nd beat. ♯ to G : om Drex. (46) ♯ to F and G : om Drex. (56) rh. ♯ : om Drex. (59) ♯ to F and G : om Drex. (61) both staves. ♭ : om Drex. (71) rh. ♯ to F, G and C : om Drex.

GALLIARD

(29) rh. last note. ♮ : om Drex. (49) 2nd beat, semiquavers a third lower : Drex ; lh. A for C : Drex. (52) rh. ♯ to C : om Drex.

21. PAVION AND GALLIARD in B mi

BM. Add. 30485. f. 107v, 109 ; Drexel 5612. p. 96, 98

PAVAN

(6) add ♯ to C : Drex. (11) add ♮ to E. both staves : Drex. (20) and (23) ♮ : added. (27) alto. add ♮ to E : BM. (30) 1st two beats FEFG, ABCB : Drex. (39) ♯ : om BM.; ♮ om BM. and Drex. (46) ♮ to E : om Drex. (48) tenor. trs up an octave. (51) ♭ to A : om BM ; rh. 1st and 2nd beats. semiquavers. a note higher : Drex. (52) ♯ to F : added. (53) lh. ♯ : om BM ; ♮ : om Drex. (55) ♯ and ♮ : added. (59) (60) and (61) ♮ to E : added (61) add ♯ to F : Drex. (62) om all accidentals : BM. (64) F♯ : trs up two octaves. (67) alto. AF for FD : Drex ; tenor. BF for FB : BM. (79) ♮ to E : om BM. (86) ♮ : om Drex. (92) add ♮ to E : BM.

GALLIARD

(12) bass. F : om BM. (15) alto. last note B : Drex. (22) tenor. 3rd beat. add D (minim) tied over to next bar : BM. (24) ♮ to E and B : om Drex. (30) rh ♮ : om BM.; lh. 3rd beat. G for B : BM. (31) rh. 1st beat. ♯ : om BM ; 2nd beat. ♮ to B and C : om Drex. (34) ♮ : om Drex. (44) ♮ : om Drex. (46) ♮ : om Drex. (bis)

22. PAVION AND GALLIARD in Gam ut

Drexel 5612. p. 140, 142

PAVAN

(20) ♭ : om Drex. (28) tenor. C for D : Drex. (55) alto. : Drex. (60) ♭ : om Drex (88) lh. ♯ : om Drex.

GALLIARD

(38) ♭ : om Drex. (cf. bar 46).

23. PAVEN AND GALIARD (incomplete) in Gam ut

BM. Add 30485 f.78v., 79.

PAVAN

(30) rh. last five notes. a third lower : BM. (32) ♯ : om BM.

GALLIARD

The text, of which no alternative source is known, seems defective, judged by the usual measures of the galliard. It is printed here as found in the manuscript without any suggestion as to how it might be completed. Three bars seem to be missing in the first strain and in the corresponding reprise. The second strain appears to be complete with four bars and reprise. The third strain is clearly incomplete, with a phrase of six bars followed by a reprise of seven.

(17) ♮ : om BM.

24. PAVANE AND GALLIARD in D sol re

Forster f. 96v, 99v

This composition is assigned to Byrd in the manuscript but there is no title or heading to it. The final bar of the pavan is in triple measure and leads into the galliard without a break. The single bars that follow 16 and 32 seem to serve as final bars at the conclusion of a repeat. Some doubt may be expressed as to the authenticity of this work.

PAVAN

(11) ♯ to C : added. (12) ♮ : om For., but cf bar 28. (31) ♯ to C : om For. (32) ♯ to C and ♮ to B : om For.

GALLIARD

The construction of this galliard is unusual. It has four sections. The first and fourth consists of four bars and a reprise. The second and third sections are of eight bars and reprise. Forster's manuscript seems to have been copied from a defective source. Bars 13 and 21 are reconstructed and inserted here to complete the eight-bar rhythm of the dance. The balance of the bass part, quite apart from this convention, points plainly to the omission. Similarly, three beats, appear to be missing in bars 28 to 29 and the corresponding bars 36 to 37 ; and these, too, have been reconstructed tentatively and added here.

25. PAVANA AND GALIARDA in D sol re

Fitzwilliam 254, 255

PAVAN

(13) rh. add ♮ to B : Fitz. (23) rh. ♮ : om Fitz. (24) lh. ♮ to B : om Fitz. (25) ♮ : om Fitz. (40) rh. ♮ : om Fitz. (56) ♯ to F and G : om Fitz. (57) ♮ : om Fitz. (69) and (85) see below for the text in the Fitzwilliam

MS. which is identical in both these bars. The editor's reconstruction here is tentative. (86) ♮ : om Fitz. (87) ♯ to C (bis) and ♮ to B : om Fitz. (94) ♮ : om Fitz. (95) lh. ♯ : om Fitz.

bars 69 and 85. Fitzwilliam

GALLIARD

(5) rh. ♭ : om Fitz. (8) ♯ : om Fitz. (16) ♮ : om Fitz. (20) 2nd chord. add ♮ to B : Fitz, but cf bar 28 (21) ♭ : om Fitz. (23) ♮ : om Fitz. (24) lh. ♯ : om Fitz. (25) ♮ : om Fitz. (30) both hands. ♮ to B, and ♭ to E : om Fitz.

26. LADY MONTEGLE'S PAVEN
Fitzwilliam 294

(51) tenor. crotchet for minim : Fitz. (54) ♯ : om Fitz. (but cf bar 66). (66) rh. ♯ : om Fitz. (67) rh. 1st beat. ♯ : om Fitz.

27. PAVIN in Gam ut
Forster f. 65v

In the third section the reprise has scarcely any variation of the theme.
(64) alto. AB for BA : For. (75) bass D for E : For.

28. PAVANA in Gam ut
Fitzwilliam 256

The third section, like the first two, consists of sixteen bars, but it has no reprise.
(38) rh. G semibreve for two minims ; and crotchet minim for minim crotchet : Fitz : tenor. 4th beat. a third lower : Fitz. (41) tenor. D for E : Fitz. (47) semiquavers all a tone lower, and last note C for A : Fitz. (48) ♯ to G : added. (53) to (56) see below. The present editor has not succeeded in reaching any satisfactory conclusion as to what the original text may have been. (64) see below. The suggested reconstruction is founded upon bars 47 to 48.

bars 53 to 56. Fitzwilliam

bar 64. Fitzwilliam

29. GALIARDO
" Mris Marye Brownlo "
Parthenia 5

This Galliard must be played in very slow time. Crowded with notes, as it is, there must never be any feeling of hurry in performance.

(37) lh. ♯ : om Parth.

30. GALIARDO SECUNDO
" Mris Marye Brownlo "
Parthenia 8. Ch. Ch. 431 f. 6v (without ascription)

Unlike the previous piece there is no reprise to any of the three strains of this galliard.
(16) lh. last chord. a third too high : Parth. (24) ♯ to F and G : om Ch. Ch.

31. Sr Jhon Grayes Galiard
Fitzwilliam 191

(15) rh. ED for DC : Fitz.

32. The Galliard Gygg
Nevell 7

This is the title given by Baldwin in the Table of Contents at the end of the Nevell book. It denotes a gigg, or jig, written in the form of a galliard. " A Galliard's Gygge ", as it is entitled in the body of the book, is evidently a transcriber's error and makes no sense. The character of a jig is shown in the rhythm of dotted crotchet-quaver, notably in bars 49 to 51. The form is that of the galliard. It is in eight sections each consisting of four bars with reprise. The bass of the first strain is repeated in the fifth ; that of the second strain in the fourth, sixth and eighth. The bass of the third strain resembles the first with some small differences, as also does the seventh.

(35) rh. 2nd beat. B. for C : N. (43) ♯ to F : om N. (59) ♯ to F : om N.

33. Galliard in Gam ut
Forster f. 95v

This is wrongly described as a pavan in the catalogue of the King's Music Library (BM.). It is plainly in the form of a galliard.

(14) rh. 2nd note. A. altered from G : For. (17) ♭ added to the signature in this line only : For. (37) and (45) 1st note E : ♭ added.

34. Galliard in Gam ut
*Forster f.*162v

35. Galliard in D sol re
Fitzwilliam 164

This galliard has sometimes been associated with the alman that is placed next before it in the Fitzwilliam book. The two pieces are independent compositions, unconnected with each other, and in different keys.

(4) ♮ to B : om Fitz. (19) ♯ to G and F : om Fitz. (27) ♯ to G and F : om Fitz. (29) 3rd beat 1st note. G for A : Fitz. (cf bar 21). (37) ♮ : om Fitz.

36. Galliard
(a fragment)
Ch. Ch. 1175. *f.* 20v

This fragment has the appearance of a transcription from lute-tablature. It is clearly in the measure of a galliard although in the manuscript it is barred in duple measures. The text is inaccurate, and it has here been slightly amended ; but the details in so unimportant a fragment as this do not call for notice.

37. Pavan and Galiarda
" Delighte : Edward Jhonson : sett by Will Byrd "
Fitzwilliam 277, 278 : *Forster f.* 139v (*pavan only*)

PAVAN

(7) 4th beat. add ♮ to F : Fitz. (13) and (14) ♮ to E : om For. (17) ♮ and ♯ : om For. (22) 3rd beat. B for C : For. (24) F♯ : om Fitz. (31) ♮ to E and ♯ to F : added. (32) ♮ : om Fitz. (40) ♮ to B : om For. (41) ♮ to B : om Fitz. (43) ♯ to F : om Fitz (bis). (55) tenor. ♮ : om Fitz.; six semi for demisemiquavers ; For ; also in bars 58, 62 and 71. (58) see below. (62) 3rd ♯ : om For. (71) lh. D for F, and D for C : For. (94) semiquavers for quavers : Fitz. (96) this bar is omitted : Fitz. (99) add ♮ to E (bis) : For.

bar 58. Forster

GALLIARD

(8) ♮ and ♯ : added. (13) lh. ♮ to E : added. (15) ♮ to E : om For. (16) DB♮ (minims) : om Fitz. (21) tenor. add ♯ to F : Fitz. (29) tenor. add ♯ to F and ♮ to E : Fitz.

38. PAVANA
" Lachrymae : Jhon Dowland : set foorth by Byrd "
Fitzwilliam 121 ; *Forster f.* 167

This piece must not be confused with settings of the same subject by Morley and Farnaby.

(16) ♮ and ♯ : om For (20) ♮ : om For. (24) lh. add ♯ to F : For. (32) ♮ : om For. (38) lh. AB for BC : For. (46) tenor. A for F : For. (47) 1st beat. ♮ : om Fitz.; last note ♮ to B : om Fitz. (57) (62) and (68) six semi for demisemiquavers. For. (64) tenor. two crotchets EA : Fitz. (67) semiquavers for four quavers : For. (80) ♯ to C : om Fitz. (81) lh. ♯ : om Fitz. (84) ♭ : om Fitz. (85) lh. ♯ to C : om For. (86) rh. 1st beat. ♯ : om For. (88) alto. semiquavers for quavers : For. (90) ♯ : added. (92) last group. quavers for semiquavers : For. (94) 2nd beat. om For.

39. GALIARDA
" James Harding : sett foorth by William Byrd "
Fitzwilliam 122 ; *Forster f.*167

(3) rh. add ♯ to F : Fitz. (cf bar 11). (37) add ♯ to G (cf bar 45) : Fitz. (47) rh. ♯ and ♮ : om Fitz.

40.   PYPER'S GALLIARD
" If my complaints. Dowland. sett foorth by Byrd "
Ch. Ch. 431, *f.*19

This is the only setting of this melody definitely attributed to Byrd. The settings in the Forster book and in the Drexel manuscript 5612 are different compositions and are not attributed to Byrd.

(9) and (10) ♭ : om Ch. Ch. (13) 2nd beat. ♯ : om Ch. Ch. (23) and (31) lh. add ♮ to E : Ch. Ch. (cf the lute tablature of Dowland). (42) ♭ to E : om Ch. Ch. (bis). (47) ♭ : om Ch. Ch.

1. THE FIRSTE PAVIAN AND GALLIARDE

2.

THE GALLIARDE

2. THE SECONDE PAVIAN AND GALLIARDE

Reprise

3.

Reprise

GALLIARDE

3. THE THIRD PAVIAN AND GALLIARDE

Moderate speed
= about 120

p

9

Reprise
17

mf

Reprise

GALLIARD

4. THE FOURTH PAVIAN AND GALLIARDE

Reprise

GALLIARD

5. THE FIFTE PAVIAN AND GALLIARDE

3

GALLIARDE

6. PAVANA THE SIXTE AND GALLIARDE

'Kinbrugh (Kinlough): goodd'

GALLIARD

7. THE SEVENTH PAVIAN
'Pavana canon'

3.

Reprise

no galliard is attached to this pavan

8. THE EIGHTE PAVIAN

3.

no galliard is attached to this pavan

9. THE NYNTHE PAVIAN AND GALLIARDE

'The Passinge Mesures'

Reprise

GALLIARD
'Galiardas Passamezzo'

Reprise (b)

10. THE TENNTHE PAVIAN AND GALLIARDE

'M! W. Peter'

Reprise
81

THE GALLIARDE

a little slower

Reprise

11. PAVANA AND GALIARDA
'Bray'

GALIARDA

12. PAVANA AND GALIARDO
The Earle of Salisbury

GALIARDO

13. PAVANA AND GALLIARD
Ph. Tr[egian]

Reprise

GALIARDA

64

14. THE QUADRAN PAVEN AND GALIARD

6 Reprise

GALLIARD
to the Quadran Paven

Reprise

Reprise

15. PAVANA AND GALLIARDA
in Gam ut

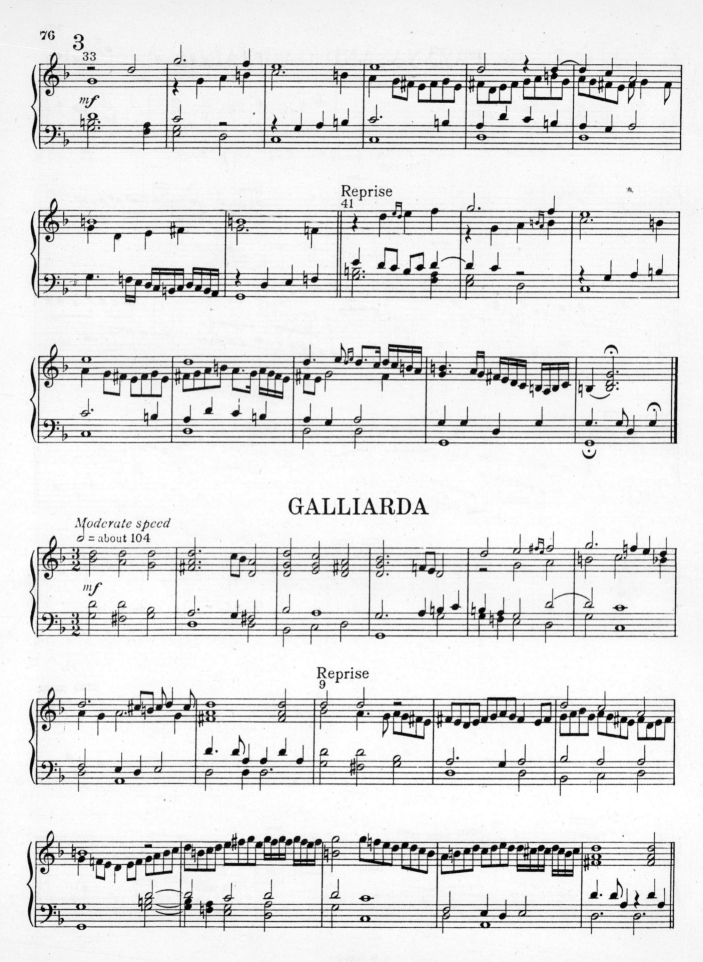

GALLIARDA

Moderate speed
♩ = about 104

16. PAVEN AND GALIARD

in Gam ut

GALLIARD

Moderate speed
♩ = about 132

mf

Reprise

2

17. PAVION AND GALLIARD
in Gam ut

GALLIARD

With movement
$\quad$ = about 144

Reprise

18. PAVANA AND GALLIARDA
in A re

GALLIARDE

19. PAVYN AND GALIARD
in A re

Reprise

GALLIARD

Reprise

20. PAVON AND GALLIARD

in A re

GALLIARD

Reprise
A little slower

21. PAVION AND GALLIARD

in B mi

GALLIARD

22. PAVION AND GALLIARD
in Gam ut

Reprise

A little slower

GALLIARD

Moderate speed
♩ = about 120

mf

Reprise

23. PAVAN AND GALIARD
in Gam ut (incomplete)

GALIARD
(apparently incomplete)

24. PAVANE AND GALLIARD

in D sol re

Reprise

Reprise

Reprise

25. PAVANA AND GALIARDA

in D sol re

GALIARDA

26. LADY MONTEGLE'S PAVEN

27. PAVIN
in Gam ut

28. PAVANA
in Gam ut

29. GALIARDO
'M^ris Marye Brownlo'

30. GALIARDO SECUNDO

'Mᴿⁱˢ Marye Brownlo'

31. Sr. JHON GRAYES GALIARD

32. THE GALLIARD GYGG

Reprise

Reprise

33. GALLIARD
in Gam ut

Very moderate speed
𝅗𝅥 = about 108

34. GALLIARD

in Gam ut

35. GALLIARD
in D sol re

Reprise

36. GALLIARD

(a fragment)

37. PAVAN AND GALIARDA

'Delighte: Edward Jhonson: sett by Will. Byrd'

GALIARDA

38. PAVANA LACHRYMAE
'Jhon Dowland: sett foorth by Byrd'

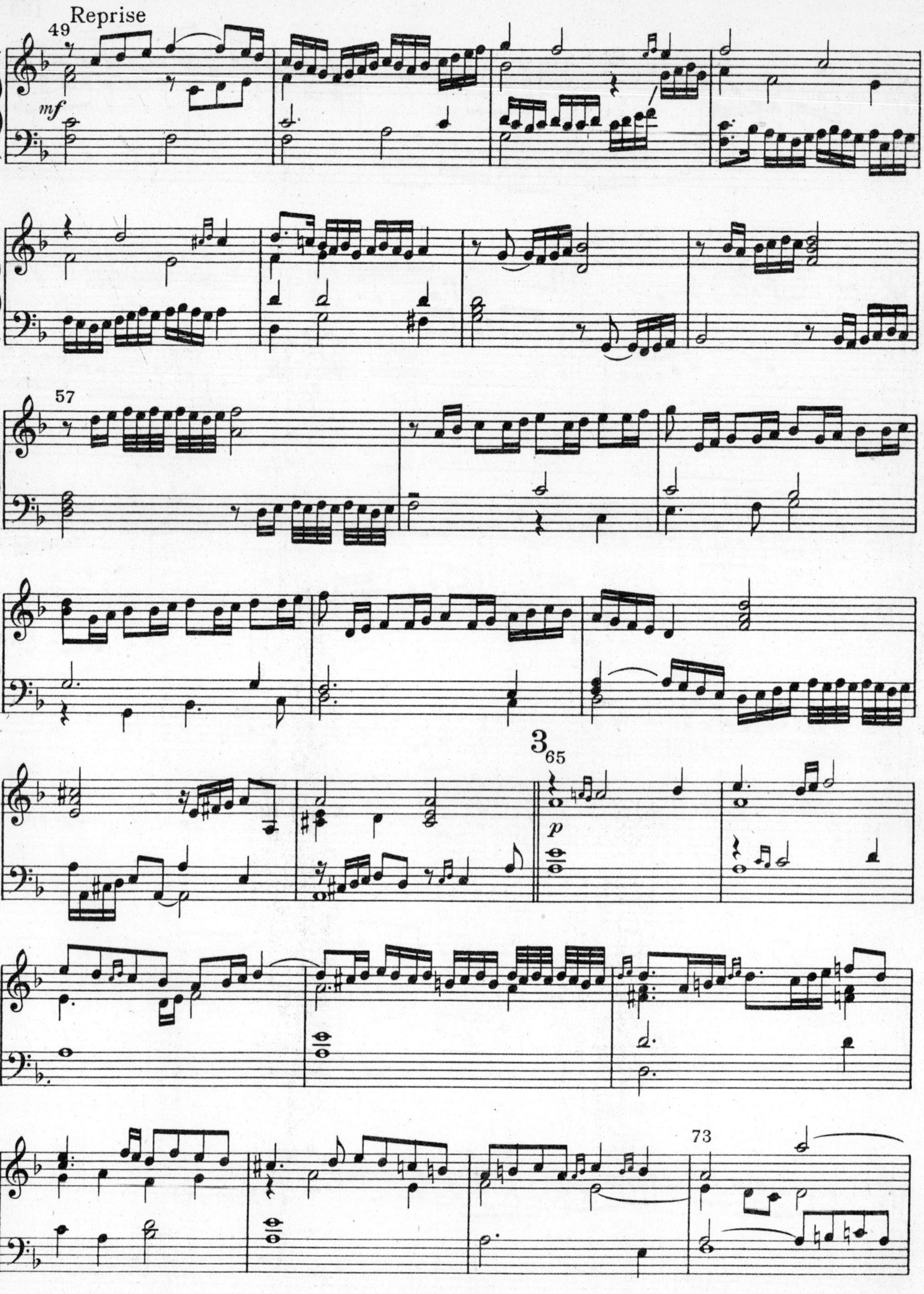
Reprise
49
mf
57
3
65
p
73

39. GALIARDA

'James Harding: sett foorth by William Byrd'

2

Reprise

40. PYPER'S GALLIARD

'If my complaints'. Dowland: sett foorth by Byrd

LOWE & BRYDONE PRINTERS LTD., LONDON